For Jack
~N.G.

For Granny & Grandad
~V.C.

TIGER TALES
An imprint of ME Media LLC
202 Old Ridgefield Road, Wilton, Connecticut 06897
First published in the United States 2001
Originally published in Great Britain 2000 by
Little Tiger Press, London
Text © 2000 Nigel Gray
Illustrations © 2000 Vanessa Cabban
CIP Data is available • ISBN 1-58925-008-7
First American edition • Printed in Belgium
All rights reserved
1 3 5 7 9 10 8 6 4 2

Little Bear's Grandpa

by NIGEL GRAY
Illustrated by VANESSA CABBAN

tiger tales

Every Friday, Little Bear went to see his grandfather.
"How's my favorite little bear?" Grandpa always asked.

"Good," said Little Bear. "And how is my favorite grandpa?"

"Just as good as an old grandpa could be," Grandpa replied.

Every Friday they had a snack together, and Little Bear looked out of the window at Grandpa's garden. In the garden was a very big, very old tree. And in the tree was a wooden platform that Grandpa called the Tree House.

Grandad kept a ladder leaning there, so that he and Little Bear could climb up to the Tree House.

After their snack Grandpa and Little Bear always climbed up into the Tree House and, sitting side by side, they looked out at the world.

"Life is a gift, Little Bear," Grandpa said. "Don't waste it."

And Little Bear replied, "I'll try not to, Grandpa. I'll do my best."

"Doing your best is the best any bear can do," said Grandpa.

From the Tree House they could see Grandpa's garden, which was green and overgrown. Grandpa called it the Jungle.

They could see a grassy hill with three gray boulders on it. Grandpa called it the Three Bears Hill.

They could see a river that twisted and turned through the valley and changed color with the weather. At sunset it sometimes looked golden and Grandpa called it Goldilocks River.

They could see an old factory chimney. Grandpa had worked in that factory when he was young. He called it the Factory of Lost Youth. But no smoke came from that chimney anymore.

Grandpa and Little Bear climbed up into the Tree House when it was sunny . . .

. . . and when it was windy . . .

. . . and when it rained— as long as it didn't rain *too* hard.

They even went there when snow lay on the ground. They took cardboard to sit on — but they never stayed too long.

And every Friday, as they sat comfortably on the platform in the tree, Little Bear said, "Tell me a story, Grandpa."

And Grandpa told stories of when he was young.

And Little Bear listened and was just as happy as he could be.

But one Friday Little Bear went to see his grandpa and Grandpa said, "I'm sorry, Little Bear. I can't come out today."
 Grandpa sat in his chair and Little Bear perched on the arm, and Grandpa told Little Bear a story about when he had been just a little bear himself.

The following Friday Little Bear didn't go to Grandpa's house. Instead, Little Bear's mother took him to the hospital. There he found Grandpa lying in bed.

"You're lazy, Grandpa," said Little Bear.

"I *am* lazy," said Grandpa. "I haven't been up all day."

Little Bear's mother went to talk to the doctor while Little Bear sat on Grandpa's bed and held his paw.

"Tell me a story, Grandpa," said Little Bear.

"I'm sorry, I'm too tired," Grandpa said. "Why don't you tell *me* a story instead."

So Little Bear told a story about a little bear who went to visit his grandpa every Friday, and how they always climbed into a tree house in Grandpa's garden. And he described all the things they could see.

When he had finished his story, Little Bear asked, "Did you like that story, Grandpa?"

But Grandpa didn't reply.

Little Bear's mother came, and she called a nurse. And the nurse called a doctor.

Then Little Bear's mother told Little Bear that Grandpa had fallen into the very deepest of deep, deep sleeps.

"When will he wake up?" asked Little Bear.

Little Bear's mother put her arms around Little Bear and held him tight.

"He won't wake up," she said.

Little Bear and his mother went back to Grandpa's house.

They climbed the ladder up to the wooden platform in the tree.

They sat together, and cried quietly, and hugged each other, looking out at the well-known things they could see.

Then, between sobs and sniffles, Little Bear said, "When I'm a grandpa, I want to be as nice a grandpa as my grandpa was to me."

"You will be, Little Bear," his mother said. "You will be."